Author: Sebastian Sarapuu
ISBN HARDBACK: 978-1-80561-069-4
ISBN PAPERBACK: 978-1-80561-630-6

Chasing Fleeting Shadows

In the twilight glow of night,
Whispers dance in soft moonlight.
Shadows stretch and fade away,
Chasing dreams that drift and sway.

The stars above are bright and bold,
Stories of the night unfold.
With every step, we lose the trace,
Of moments that we can't replace.

Fleeting shadows, whispers near,
Echoes of our lingering fear.
Through the night, they come and go,
Filling hearts with soft, sweet glow.

Time slips by, like grains of sand,
Gone too soon, we never planned.
Yet in the chase, there's beauty found,
In every haunting, hushed sound.

Dandelion Wishes on a Breezy Day

Blown by winds, the wishes fly,
Dandelions dance against the sky.
Children laugh and chase the seeds,
Filling hearts with hopeful needs.

With each puff, a dream takes flight,
Glittering gold in morning light.
Tender hopes in gentle hands,
Carried forth to distant lands.

The breeze whispers secrets sweet,
Promises in each heartbeat.
Wishful thoughts on wings of air,
Carried high without a care.

Moments brief, yet ever dear,
Captured in the child's cheer.
Dandelion wishes softly fade,
To memories the breeze has laid.

Echoing Silence of Souvenirs

Dusty shelves hold stories old,
Whispers of adventures told.
Souvenirs of laughter, tears,
Echo softly through the years.

Photographs in frames of gold,
Memories that never fold.
Each silence hides a gentle sigh,
A testament of days gone by.

Letters penned in ink and pain,
Each word speaks of joy and rain.
Echoing silence, bittersweet,
Guarding every heartbeat's beat.

Trinkets hold the touch of time,
Each a note, a whispered rhyme.
In stillness, they embrace the past,
Echoes of a love amassed.

The Remains of Our Serenade

Softly strummed on twilight's edge,
Music lingered, made a pledge.
Notes that danced upon the air,
Whispered truths we used to share.

Faded chords, a gentle sting,
Reminds us of the joy we bring.
In the silence, echoes play,
The remains of our serenade.

Each melody, a fleeting glance,
Carried forth in lost romance.
Ghosts of laughter, sweet refrain,
Haunting softly like the rain.

Yet in shadows, light survives,
In every note, our love derives.
Though the song may fade away,
The heart remembers the ballet.

Shattered Echoes of Affection

In fragments, love once soared high,
Now whispers fall like autumn's sigh.
The laughter dances on the breeze,
Yet sorrow clings like tangled trees.

Memories linger, shadows glance,
Faded flickers of a lost romance.
Each heartbeat feels the silent ache,
As time erodes the paths we make.

Reflections caught in crystal shards,
Of tender words that now feel hard.
We search for warmth in shadows cast,
While haunted by the ghost of past.

In every corner, time's embrace,
A whispered promise, now a trace.
Yet through the pain, we still believe,
In shattered echoes, we conceive.

Pieces of a Tender Landscape

In hues of dawn, our moments weave,
A canvas bright, too pure to leave.
Soft lavender and shades of blue,
A tender landscape, me and you.

The petals fall as seasons change,
Yet every memory feels so strange.
Amidst the blooms, the thorns bleed through,
A gentle touch, but pain anew.

With every heartbeat, we explore,
The pieces left upon the floor.
A tapestry, frayed at the seams,
Yet woven deep with whispered dreams.

In quiet corners, love's refrain,
The echoes linger, joy and pain.
Yet through the struggle, we will find,
A landscape tender, redefined.

Whispers in the Cracks of Love

Upon the walls where shadows play,
Whispers echo, night and day.
In silent crevices of trust,
We search for hope, as lovers must.

The moonlight casts its silver hue,
On cracks that hold our memories true.
In every whisper, secrets sigh,
Beneath the weight of a heartfelt cry.

Fleeting glimpses through the haze,
Of tender moments lost in a daze.
Yet every echo sings a song,
Of love that's deep, enduring strong.

Through broken lines, our stories merge,
In whispered prayers, our spirits surge.
For in the cracks, we learn to see,
The beauty of what's meant to be.

The Mosaic of Memory

Each shard reflects a different hue,
A mosaic crafted, me and you.
In pieces formed from joy and pain,
A tapestry that will remain.

The vibrant stories clash and blend,
As time's brush strokes, curves, and bends.
Within the chaos, still we find,
The art of love, uniquely blind.

With every facet, light will dance,
Transforming sorrow into chance.
In broken patterns, we create,
A memory we celebrate.

In whispers soft, our journeys chart,
The threads of life, a work of art.
For in this mosaic, we shall see,
The beauty of our history.

Where Shadows Dance

In twilight's glow, the shadows sway,
Whispering secrets of the day.
Figures blur in the soft embrace,
Where dreams and silence find their space.

Beneath the trees, the whispers call,
In the dark, we rise, we fall.
Every movement, a fleeting chance,
In this realm where shadows dance.

Moonlight glimmers on the ground,
A serenade, a haunting sound.
Every step, a rhythm shared,
In a world where few have dared.

The stars above begin to play,
Lighting paths for those who stray.
In the calm, where hearts entrust,
We find our peace among the dust.

When dawn arrives, the shadows fade,
Yet in our hearts, the echoes laid.
In memories' grip, we shall enhance,
The fleeting magic of our dance.

Unraveled Threads

Tangled fibers tell a tale,
Of moments lost beneath the veil.
Each strand a memory we weave,
In the quiet, we grieve and cleave.

Through the years, the fibers fray,
Each thread a whisper of yesterday.
As time unravels what we hold,
Stories fade like threads of gold.

A tapestry rich with hopes and dreams,
Now a puzzle of lost seams.
With every pull, a piece gives way,
Leaving shadows of what we say.

In the silence, we mend and sew,
Reweaving paths we used to know.
Yet some threads, they cannot bind,
In the gaps, the truths unwind.

So we gather what we can,
From the remnants of our plan.
In the fabric of life, we thread,
Our stories live, though some are dead.

The Remnants of Us

Fragments linger in the air,
Echoes of laughter we used to share.
Distant memories softly hum,
Remnants of us, where love begun.

In every corner, shadows play,
Holding onto what slipped away.
Golden moments now turned gray,
In the silence, we yearn to stay.

Faded photographs, time-worn pages,
Chronicles of our fleeting stages.
In the heart, the stories dwell,
In the gaps, we weave our spell.

Yet in the dusk, hope finds a way,
To light the path of yesterday.
Though distance stretches like a vast sea,
The remnants of us forever be.

So let us stroll through lost avenues,
Gather the fragments we choose to use.
In every whisper, a past we trust,
In the ashes, we find the just.

Echoing Silence

In the stillness, thoughts collide,
An echoing silence, a space to hide.
Words unspoken, heavy air,
In the quiet, we find our despair.

The distance stretches, a vast divide,
With every heartbeat, hope has died.
Yet in the hush, a promise lingers,
A faint light born from trembling fingers.

Through the void, our dreams take flight,
Carried softly into the night.
In every pause, a truth is found,
As whispers rise from hollow ground.

Listen close, the silence sings,
A melody of forgotten things.
In its embrace, we search for peace,
In echoing silence, find release.

For in stillness, the soul can mend,
Through silent battles, we transcend.
In every heartbeat's steady dance,
We'll find our way, our sacred chance.

Unruly Hearts

In the shadows where whispers dwell,
Beat the hearts that never tell.
Caught in storms of fervent fire,
Dancing dreams that never tire.

Wild like vines that twist and grow,
Yearning souls that ebb and flow.
Holding tight, but wanting free,
Unruly hearts in harmony.

Amidst the chaos, laughter sings,
Beneath the weight of fragile things.
Through the night, they find their way,
Chasing dawn, dispelling gray.

Fragile hopes that may ignite,
Stars in darkness, fierce and bright.
Boundless love, a reckless dart,
Living bold with unruly heart.

In the silence, secrets creep,
While we wander, while we leap.
Through tangled paths, we'll always roam,
Finding in each other, home.

Weaving Through Broken Threads

In the loom of days gone by,
Frayed edges whisper, sigh.
Each thread a lesson, stitched in pain,
A tapestry of joy and rain.

Patterns form in shades of gray,
Colors blend, then fade away.
Weaving dreams with gentle hands,
Mending hearts, stitching strands.

Each knot a story, deep and true,
Binding hope with every hue.
Every tear, a tale retold,
Of warmth found in threads of gold.

Through the fabric, life unfolds,
In each seam, a memory holds.
Fragile fibers hold us tight,
In the dark, they weave us light.

As we twine through time's embrace,
Lost in every scar, every trace.
We find solace, our way ahead,
Weaving through broken threads.

The Weight of a Word

Words like feathers, soft and light,
Can pierce the heart, ignite the night.
With gentle tones, they heal the soul,
Or split apart, a wounded whole.

A whisper shared, a promise made,
In silence held, our hopes conveyed.
Yet careless tongues can cause much pain,
A simple phrase can leave a stain.

In laughter's ring, they dance and play,
In sorrow's sigh, they drift away.
Every utterance, a choice we bear,
The weight of words hangs in the air.

Through love's embrace, they find their place,
In every smile, a warm embrace.
Each syllable a fleeting light,
Guiding us through darkest night.

Let us choose with tender care,
For words can change the world we share.
With kindness, let our voices soar,
For in a word, we hold much more.

Lost in the Pages

In quiet corners, stories lie,
Ink-stained dreams, beneath the sky.
Pages whisper tales of old,
Of heroes brave and hearts of gold.

Through winding plots, we find our way,
In every line, the words convey.
Trapped in chapters, shadows play,
Lost in the pages, here we'll stay.

Time stands still as pages turn,
In every heartbreak, lessons learn.
Each character, a piece of heart,
Unlocking worlds where hopes depart.

Ink and paper weave a spell,
Transporting us where wonders dwell.
Among the lines of fate's design,
We discover love's sweet sign.

So take a journey, turn the page,
Get lost in time, uncage the sage.
For in these tales, we're never alone,
In ink and dreams, we find our home.

Shattered Whispers

Whispers in the night,
Flicker like dim stars.
Echoing the silence,
Carrying hidden scars.

Fragments of a voice,
Lost in the cool air.
Dreams of secret choices,
Falling unaware.

Caught in a still pause,
Truth becomes a feign.
Glimmers of the past,
Pierce through like the rain.

Sifting through the dust,
Memories collide.
Shattered bits of hope,
With nowhere to hide.

Yet, amidst the ruins,
Sprouts a fragile light.
Guided by the shards,
We rise in the night.

Echoes of Emotion

A heart filled with longing,
Beneath a silver moon.
Soft echoes of laughter,
Haunting every room.

Tides of sweet reminiscence,
Crashing on the shore.
Waves of joy and sorrow,
Kissing us once more.

Thoughts swirl like the wind,
Dancing in the dark.
Lighting up the shadows,
Fueling every spark.

Moments fade like whispers,
In the chilling air.
Yet they linger softly,
Like perfume, rare.

In echoes of the past,
We find what we seek.
Threads of emotion,
Make the spirit speak.

Pieces of a Broken Dream

Scattered like confetti,
Empty promises fall.
Fragments of a vision,
Echoing the call.

A canvas now in shambles,
Colors lost to time.
Brushstrokes turned to shadows,
Chiming a sad rhyme.

But in the broken bits,
Stories still remain.
Whispers of the future,
Hiding in the pain.

With every shattered piece,
A lesson unfolds clear.
From the depths of darkness,
Hope can persevere.

So gather up the shards,
Embrace them, don't resist.
For in the broken dream,
A brand new chance exists.

The Tattered Edges of Love

Frayed threads of passion,
Whisper secrets low.
Tenderness now faded,
But the feelings glow.

In the tattered corners,
Love's imprint remains.
Crumbling like old paper,
Yet it still sustains.

Hands that once held tightly,
Now drift far apart.
Yet the warmth of memory,
Lives within the heart.

With every single tear,
A new stitch is made.
We patch up what we've lost,
In the light and shade.

So love, though it may fray,
Finds strength in the binds.
In tattered edges, hope,
Awaits what love finds.

Splintered Promises

In whispers soft, they fade away,
Shattered dreams in disarray.
Echoes linger, haunt the night,
Hope now lost, out of sight.

Once we soared on wings of grace,
Now we stumble, fall from place.
Fingers touch, yet drift apart,
Splintered vows, a broken heart.

Memories dance, like shadows cast,
Remnants of a love that couldn't last.
Each memory a thorny rose,
Beauty lies in pain that grows.

Time won't mend what fate has frayed,
In the silence, sorrow swayed.
Promises like glass, they shatter,
Leaving only empty chatter.

Still I hope, despite the pain,
To find a way to love again.
But for now, I mourn the spark,
In the echoes of the dark.

Chasing Starlit Hearts

We chase the stars in velvet skies,
With dreams that glimmer in our eyes.
Holding hands, we make a vow,
In this moment, here and now.

Mysterious lights guide our way,
Through the night, to break of day.
The universe whispers our names,
In a dance of cosmic flames.

Wishes whispered on the breeze,
Like the rustling of the trees.
With every heartbeat, we draw near,
Lost in love, we've no more fear.

We paint our story in the sky,
With every laugh, a gentle sigh.
Starlit dreams, they twirl and spin,
In this journey, love begins.

Though shadows linger, hope remains,
In the night, we fight the chains.
Forever chasing, side by side,
Two starlit hearts, in love we bide.

Tainted Joy

In laughter's clutch, a shadow hides,
A taint of sorrow, joy abides.
Smiles that mask the tears we cry,
A fleeting glance, a heavy sigh.

Moments stolen, joy entwined,
In the darkness, light's defined.
We dance beneath the silver moon,
Yet silence hums a haunting tune.

Fragile hearts, they wear a mask,
In every joy, a hidden task.
Finding peace in muted cries,
While laughter fades, the spirit flies.

Tainted joy, a bittersweet,
In every smile, a chance to meet.
Yet still we rise, we seek the glow,
In every shadow, love will flow.

Though burdens press, we'll find our way,
Through the night to greet the day.
In hearts unbroken, hope will nudge,
We'll turn the pain to sweetest grudge.

Lost in the Tides of Time

We drift like shadows on the shore,
The waves of memory, we explore.
Each tide pulls us, whispers low,
Where did the fleeting moments go?

In the sands of time, we write our fate,
With every ebb, we contemplate.
Fragments swirl in salty air,
Once vivid dreams, now laid bare.

Fading echoes of laughter's light,
In the depth of the endless night.
Gone are the days, but not the pain,
As tides return, so does the rain.

Frozen moments chart the course,
In the ocean's depths lies our source.
We'll search the swell, through dark and deep,
To find the secrets that we keep.

Lost in time, yet hope still shines,
In every wave, our love reminds.
We'll sail again, through the shifts sublime,
Together, forever, lost in time.

Silhouettes of a Love Once Known

In shadows cast by fading light,
Two hearts embraced, now out of sight.
Memories whisper, secrets shared,
A love once bright, now lightly bared.

Ghostly figures sway and dance,
In twilight's glow, a fleeting chance.
Echoes linger, soft and low,
In silhouettes, our hearts will grow.

Unraveled threads of time entwined,
In dreams, your face I seek to find.
Yet time's cruel hand doth steal away,
Leaving shadows where once we lay.

The moon bears witness to our past,
In tender moments, shadows cast.
But love's warm embers softly fade,
In silhouettes our memories braid.

Though paths may part and journeys roam,
In every heart, you find a home.
For love once known, though lost to time,
Shall linger soft in every rhyme.

Fleeting Glances in the Mist

Amidst the fog where secrets lie,
Two souls entwined, yet passing by.
In silent whispers, laughter shared,
Fleeting glances, a bond declared.

The morning dew holds tales retold,
In glimmers bright, both warm and cold.
Between the haze, your eyes find mine,
A moment brief, yet so divine.

Hands brushed softly, a spark ignites,
In tender breaths, sweetened flights.
The mist surrounds, a veil of dreams,
In every whisper, love redeems.

As shadows meld with dawning light,
We weave our wishes, taking flight.
Though paths may twist and hearts may stray,
Our fleeting glances still replay.

In every sigh, the echoes stay,
In every heart, a secret way.
Though moments fade like morning's bliss,
We'll cherish each, a fleeting kiss.

Canvas of Mended Dreams

On canvas pale, we paint our tales,
With strokes of hope where love prevails.
Each color bright, a story spun,
In every hue, our hearts are one.

Brush of time, it stroked so fine,
Merged our dreams with fate's design.
In every shade, a tear was dried,
In vibrant hues, our souls collide.

With every stroke, new paths emerge,
From gray despair, we start to surge.
Mended pieces, scars displayed,
In art we find the love we made.

The masterpiece unfolds with grace,
A gallery of hope to embrace.
In every corner, soft and bright,
Our love reflects in sheer delight.

And though the canvas bears our strife,
In every shade, we find our life.
A testament to dreams we've sewn,
In colored whispers, love has grown.

The Fray of Yesterday's Affection

In frayed edges where memories cling,
The whispers of yesterday softly sing.
Threads of affection, worn yet strong,
In tattered dreams, we still belong.

Through storms endured and trials faced,
In every heartbeat, love embraced.
The tapestry, a tale unfolds,
In vibrant hues, our hearts behold.

Though time may tangle love's sweet thread,
Resilient bonds can't be misled.
For in the fray, the heart grows bold,
In every loss, a tale retold.

With every stitch, forgiveness we sew,
In fading light, our spirits glow.
For yesterday's affection remains,
In every joy, in every pain.

So let the frayed edges gently show,
The beauty of love, as we let go.
For in each tear, a story brims,
In every shadow, our love swims.

The Anatomy of Longing

My heart aches with quiet pleas,
Chasing shadows on the breeze.
In the stillness, dreams reside,
Whispers of love, deep inside.

Each heartbeat tells its silent tale,
Wishes carried on the pale.
Fragments linger, lost and worn,
In the night, a soul reborn.

Through the distance, hope extends,
Yearning for what never ends.
An embrace that's felt, not seen,
In the space where we have been.

Fingers trace the empty air,
Longing's grip, a heavy snare.
Yet in shadows, light may bloom,
Silent love that fills the room.

With every sigh, the world retreats,
Unveiling tender, aching beats.
A map of feelings, etched in sand,
Yearning speaks when we can't stand.

Echoes of Unspoken Words

In the quiet, voices rise,
Unsaid truths beneath the skies.
Each thought dances in the dark,
Flickers bright, a hidden spark.

Caught in webs of time and space,
Hesitation leaves a trace.
Words unsaid, they linger near,
In the silence, loud and clear.

Faces turn, the past remains,
Hidden love, like gentle chains.
An embrace that never came,
Fueling the unspoken flame.

In the void where echoes play,
What we feared to say today.
Let the whispers find their way,
To the heart we wish to stay.

Conversations lost in time,
Each moment, a silent rhyme.
But in absence, feelings grow,
Unvoiced love, a steady flow.

Woven Threads of Forgotten Moments

Time unravels, threads unwind,
Moments fade but linger blind.
In the fabric of our days,
Soft reminders, gentle ways.

Each memory, a stitch we hold,
Stories shared, both warm and cold.
Faded echoes, whispers light,
In the tapestry of night.

Colors blend, yet still remain,
Joy and sorrow, love and pain.
Woven deep in every heart,
Fragments never meant to part.

Lost in time, yet here we stand,
Threads unbroken, hand in hand.
With each pulse, the fabric sways,
As we dance through endless days.

In every fold, the laughter hums,
In every tear, the heartache comes.
Woven threads of who we are,
Bright as dreams, yet dim as stars.

The Puzzle of Past Emotions

Pieces scattered, heart's lament,
Fragments of a life well spent.
Each sorrow holds a silent key,
Unlocking truths we cannot see.

In the shadows, memories play,
Faded hopes that refuse to stay.
Puzzles formed through joy and strife,
Lost connections, shades of life.

Tangled webs of what we feel,
Time reveals, but never heals.
With every breath, we seek to find,
The hidden links that bind our mind.

Yearning for a brighter hue,
In the pieces, I find you.
Though the picture may be soft,
In every loss, a chance to loft.

Through the maze, the heart may roam,
In the puzzle, we find home.
Every edge a memory's grace,
Emotions echo, time can trace.

Shadows Barely Seen

In the corners of light, they flicker,
Echoes of whispers, growing thicker.
A dance with the dusk, a fleeting trace,
Memories linger in this hidden space.

Veils of the past skimming our feet,
Where silence and shadows quietly meet.
A pause in the air, secrets confined,
Footsteps retreating, a path left behind.

Faint outlines sketch what we can't discern,
A flicker of hope, for which we yearn.
We seek in the dark for a glimpse of grace,
In shadows barely seen, we find our place.

With every heartbeat, they softly sway,
Guiding us gently, come what may.
In the mist of the night, fears may collide,
But we walk on with shadows as our guide.

Under the moon's soft glow, we weave,
Stories untold, we dare to believe.
Embracing the darkness, we find the light,
In shadows barely seen, we rise to fight.

The Color of Old Flames

Ashes settled on the cold ground,
Echoes of laughter, once profound.
Flickers of gold in the ember's glow,
Memories linger of love's warm flow.

Time passes by, yet the heart recalls,
Soft whispers of warmth through stone-walled halls.
Hues of the past painted in fire,
Color the moments that never tire.

A spark in the dark, a once-bright blaze,
Lighting the path through a smoky haze.
We chase the shadows of what used to be,
In the color of old flames, we're set free.

Through seasons that change, the flame may die,
But embers survive under the night sky.
The warmth finds a way through winter's chill,
In love's memory, we find our will.

So let us gather and tend to the spark,
Rekindle the brightness within the dark.
For even old flames can burn bright anew,
In shades of love, forever true.

Notes from a Broken Song

In the silence, a melody aches,
Fragments of rhythm that the heart breaks.
Waves of emotion crash and then settle,
The notes of the past in a heart's old metal.

A chorus of longing in shadows cast,
Echoes of laughter that cannot last.
Harmonies fade, but the pain persists,
In the silence, a song that twists.

With every heartbeat, the tremors rise,
Lost in the echoes of whispered goodbyes.
Each note a reminder of joy and despair,
In a broken song, we breathe the air.

Time moves onward, but the pain remains,
Memories linger like soft summer rains.
A ballad of life, the highs and the lows,
In notes from a broken song, the heart knows.

Yet through the sorrow, a beauty sings,
In the fractured pieces, new hope springs.
From the chaos, a symphony's dream,
In each broken note, we find a theme.

A Canvas of Lives Unlived

Brush strokes of dreams on empty white,
Stories untold that flicker with light.
Colors of courage, the palette unseen,
A canvas of lives that might have been.

Each splash a whisper of choices made,
Echoes of paths through the colors laid.
In the silence of thought, potential sighs,
Dreams left unfinished beneath the skies.

A tapestry woven with threads of chance,
Faint hopes lingering in a quiet dance.
The art of longing, a canvas wide,
With possibilities that we can't abide.

Imagination flows like a river wide,
Crafting the lives we wish to ride.
With every heartbeat, we nurture the dream,
In a canvas of lives, we strive to gleam.

So let us color this blank space bold,
With the stories of lives we dare to hold.
In the beauty of dreams, we break every mold,
On a canvas of lives unnumbered and untold.

The Language of Lost Affection

Words once spoken, now just echoes,
Whispers lost in the evening air.
Fragments of laughter, faded shadows,
Silence lingers, heavy with care.

Letters unsent, secrets unshared,
Pages turned, a story untold.
Love like a breeze, once freely bared,
Now trapped in memories, bitter and cold.

Glimmers of warmth in a winter's chill,
Hearts once open, now tightly sealed.
The language of love, a haunting thrill,
Now a ghost in the dreams we concealed.

Time moves on, but the ache remains,
In every smile, a fleeting glance.
Soft tender touch that still entertains,
The shadows of what might have been chance.

Yet in the silence, a spark ignites,
A flicker of hope within the night.
For lost affection, though it still bites,
Can bloom anew with the dawn's first light.

Dreams in Shattered Glass

Reflections break upon the floor,
Each shard a wish that slipped away.
Memories haunt like an open door,
Inviting thoughts of yesterday.

Colorful pieces, sharp yet bright,
Whisper stories of paths once walked.
In broken dreams, there lies a light,
A mosaic of victory, softly talked.

Fleeting visions in morning's glow,
Waking to find the glass is strewn.
Where once were hopes, now echoes flow,
Beneath the quiet, the lost dreams croon.

Amidst the cuts, new shapes arise,
Beauty formed from the pain we bear.
In every fracture, truth belies,
Life moves forward, nothing to spare.

With gentle hands, we learn to mend,
Crafting futures from jumbled past.
In every ending, we find a friend,
The dreams we cherish, forever cast.

Raindrops on Forgotten Paths

Gentle whispers touch the ground,
Each droplet sings a subtle song.
On paths once taken, lost but found,
Nature's rhythm, where hearts belong.

Puddles reflect a sky of grey,
Mirrored dreams in a world so vast.
In the rain's embrace, we drift away,
To moments etched in shadows cast.

Memories dance with every fall,
Footsteps traced in the softened earth.
Echoes linger, answering the call,
Of joy that springs from our heart's rebirth.

Each raindrop holds a fleeting glance,
A reminder of times we once knew.
Branches sway in a silent dance,
Nature's symphony, warm and true.

Through winding paths and tempest's grace,
We embrace the rhythm of our days.
In rainy moments, find your place,
For every journey, love always stays.

A Patch of Thorns

In a garden where roses grow,
Blooming bright with colors so bold.
Yet hidden below, where few dare go,
Lies a secret that's waiting to unfold.

Petals soft, caressed by the sun,
Entwined with shadows that whisper low.
Among the beauty, the thorns do run,
A reminder of love's bittersweet flow.

Every bloom tells a tale of pain,
Of hearts once broken, mended, scarred.
In every petal, a hint of rain,
Grief entwined with joy, forever marred.

Yet in this patch, wisdom is born,
For beauty thrives where pain has been.
Among the thorns, new life is sworn,
A testament to the strength within.

So cherish the blooms, honor the scars,
Life's garden is vast, with lessons grown.
In every thorn, beneath the stars,
We find our way, not alone.

Stories Written in the Wind

Whispers dance on gentle air,
Carrying tales from far and near.
Each breeze a secret, soft yet bold,
Revealing stories yet untold.

Leaves rustle like pages turned,
In nature's book, the fire burned.
Voices echo in the sighs,
While shadows play beneath the skies.

Clouds drift by like dreams in flight,
Scattered fragments, pure delight.
In the distance, laughter rings,
As the heart of freedom sings.

The wind carries hopes anew,
With every gust, the world feels true.
Memories woven, soft and grand,
Entwined within the golden sand.

Through valleys deep and mountains high,
The stories float, they never die.
In the whispers of the night,
The wind will tell, and hearts take flight.

Tarred Lyrics of Silence

In shadows cast, a still refrain,
Voices muffled, bound in chain.
The quiet speaks in muted tones,
Where every thought and dream atones.

Echoes linger, hidden deep,
Secrets that the stillness keep.
Each whisper lost in cosmic space,
In silence, we find our place.

Time slows down, a breath held tight,
In the darkness, sparks of light.
Melodies wrapped in fragile grace,
A gentle touch, a soft embrace.

Yet in the calm, we find our spark,
A flicker bright within the dark.
With tarred lyrics bound in lore,
The silence sings forevermore.

Beneath the weight of heavy days,
We seek the light in whispered ways.
In the depth where silence reigns,
A symphony within our veins.

Memories in the Mist

Morning fog wraps the world in grey,
Hiding moments, lost in play.
Each droplet holds a memory dear,
A fleeting smile, a silent tear.

Dancing shadows drift and sway,
In whispered dreams they find their way.
Familiar faces come and go,
In the mist, memories grow.

Footsteps echo on wet, cool ground,
In silent spaces, solace found.
The past hangs heavy like the dew,
Each breath a glimpse of what we knew.

As the sun breaks through the haze,
Golden light ignites the maze.
But still the mist reminds us all,
Of fleeting time, the rise and fall.

Hold tight the moments soft and soft,
In the mist, we soar aloft.
For every dream that we once kissed,
Lives on still, in memory's mist.

Fleeting Glances

In crowded rooms, our eyes did meet,
A moment brief, yet bittersweet.
Silent words hung in the air,
A spark ignited, a distant flare.

Across the hall, we shared a smile,
With fleeting glances, we paused a while.
Time slowed down, the world grew still,
An unspoken bond, a quiet thrill.

With every turn, I caught your gaze,
Illuminated by nostalgia's haze.
Yet life moved on, we drifted apart,
But those fleeting moments touched my heart.

In memory's frame, those looks remain,
Fragments of joy, tinged with pain.
Forever cherished, forever lost,
In the dance of time, we pay the cost.

When shadows fall and dreams take flight,
I'll hold those glances into the night.
Though paths diverge and stories end,
In fleeting moments, you were my friend.

A Symphony of Broken Notes

In a room filled with echoes of sound,
Whispers of melodies lost, unbound.
Fingers slip on the dusty keys,
A symphony born from forgotten pleas.

The trumpet cries with its tangled tune,
A serenade to the somber moon.
Notes drift like leaves in the autumn air,
Each one a story, a burden to bear.

Strings vibrate softly, a tear in the past,
Melancholic whispers, shadows cast.
Each pause a memory, each chord a sigh,
In this symphony, dreams come to die.

Harmonies clash like waves on the shore,
A tempest of feelings that minds can't ignore.
Yet within the chaos, a beauty shines bright,
In broken notes, we find our light.

So I play my heart on this fragile stage,
With hope that the music will turn a new page.
In the symphony's end, we find our peace,
Among the broken, our souls release.

Collaged Affection

Pieces of us in colors collide,
Fragments of laughter engulfing our stride.
In silent whispers, our stories unfold,
A patchwork of moments, cherished and bold.

Each photograph holds a slice of time,
Captured in frames, like verses in rhyme.
With memories pasted in red and blue,
Together we crafted this tapestry true.

Sticky fingers from glue and from cheer,
We stitched together all we hold dear.
In every corner, a memory shines,
A collage of love, where our heart aligns.

Time may weather the pages we hold,
But the warmth of our laughter will never grow old.
In every crease, there's a grin and a sigh,
In this collage of affection, you and I.

So let's keep crafting, layer by layer,
With each fleeting moment, I'll always care.
In this art of us, I find my refrain,
Collaged affection, like love in the rain.

Distant Echoes of Laughter

Fading laughter in the evening light,
Echoes of joy take their quiet flight.
Underneath stars where shadows play,
Memories linger, stubborn to stay.

Down cobblestone paths, we used to roam,
Finding our way, no need for a home.
Each giggle, a spark, igniting the air,
In distant echoes, I still find you there.

Years may pass like a fleeting breeze,
Yet in the whispers, my heart finds ease.
For laughter binds us even apart,
A timeless embrace, a shared beating heart.

With every smile that flits through the night,
I catch fleeting glimmers of pure delight.
In stillness, I hear that joyous refrain,
The distant echoes, a sweet, soft gain.

So here in the twilight, I pause and reflect,
On moments so cherished, I'll never reject.
Though laughter may fade, its warmth will remain,
In the distant echoes, love knows no chain.

Frayed Paths of Connection

In shadows cast by yesterday's light,
We wander through memories, lost in flight.
With every step, the threads unwind,
Frayed paths of connection, hard to find.

Words once spoken hang in the air,
Echoes of moments, a silent stare.
We trace the lines where silence grew,
A canvas painted in shades of blue.

Yet in the distance, hope does gleam,
A fractured bond, a whispering dream.
We gather the shards, we start to mend,
A journey anew, where hearts can blend.

Through storms we've weathered, in twilight's glow,
We learn to dance in a softer flow.
Together we rise, hand in hand,
Frayed paths of connection, together we stand.

Echoes in a Hollow Space

In the chamber of memories, whispers reside,
Fade like a moment, where shadows collide.
Each heartbeat lingers, a strong embrace,
Yet we are left with echoes in a hollow space.

Walls speak the tales of laughter and tears,
Ghosts of the past weave through the years.
In silence we search for the words not said,
In the hollowness, paths of our dread.

Time, the thief, with its gentle hand,
Steals what was once in our weary land.
But whispers of hope still flicker and glow,
In echoes we find what we didn't know.

Perhaps in the quiet, there's beauty undisclosed,
In hollowed spaces, our hearts are exposed.
We gather the pieces, we make our own way,
Echoes resound, guiding night into day.

Ghosts of Laughter

In the corners of rooms where laughter once soared,
Now only silence, the ghosts are ignored.
Memories linger, a bittersweet breeze,
Carrying whispers through swaying trees.

A playful snicker floats in the air,
Reminders of moments when joy sparked care.
Yet shadows encroach where light used to dance,
As ghosts of laughter fade with a glance.

We search for the echoes, the joyful refrain,
In photographs faded, in sunshine and rain.
For in the lightness, we find our way back,
To the places where joy never did lack.

So let us remember the smiles we once shared,
For laughter's true strength is never ensnared.
In the depths of our hearts, let those giggles remain,
Ghosts of laughter, forever sustain.

The Jigsaw of Love's End

Pieces once fitting, a colorful scene,
Now scattered and broken, hints of what's been.
With edges frayed, we search for the part,
In the jigsaw of love, we mend a lost heart.

Each moment a fragment, a story to tell,
Some fit together, while others repel.
As we find our way through the shards on the floor,
We learn the art of loving once more.

Time shows us beauty in patterns of pain,
The end of a puzzle can teach us to gain.
In spaces unfilled, new shapes arise,
The jigsaw of love, under brightening skies.

Though pieces may stray, they lead to a whole,
In each twist and turn, we discover our role.
With courage and grace, we piece it again,
In the jigsaw of love, there's always a gain.

Reflections of a Silenced Heart

In shadows deep, my thoughts reside,
A heart once loud, now whispers wide.
Echoes linger, soft and low,
Silent songs the soul won't show.

With every tear, a story spun,
Winds of change, the battles won.
Through the quiet, strength will find,
The whispered hopes of a muted mind.

Lost in dreams, the past unfolds,
Faded moments, secrets told.
A canvas painted in shades of grace,
Reflections found in time and space.

Yet still I breathe, though shadows press,
In silence, there's a quietness.
The heart may ache, yet yearns to sing,
In every pause, a possibility's wing.

The Unraveled Quilt

Threads of memory intertwine,
Stitched together, yours and mine.
Colors fade, yet warmth remains,
In every patch, laughter's stains.

Each square a life, a tale to weave,
Patterns rich, we choose to leave.
A fabric worn with love and care,
Whispers held in every layer.

Time may fray the edges slight,
But stories glow with gentle light.
A quilt of dreams, both old and new,
Each thread a heartbeat shared by two.

Beneath the stars, we lay it wide,
Underneath, the truth won't hide.
Together wrapped in tender grace,
We find our solace in this space.

A Journey Untold

With every step, the road unfolds,
A path of wonder, tales retold.
Mountains high and valleys deep,
In every stride, the secrets keep.

Whispers call from distant shores,
Dreams await through open doors.
Footprints left on sands of time,
Echoes of a future rhyme.

Stars above guide the way,
Through night's embrace and light of day.
A heart that dares, a soul that seeks,
In every silence, courage speaks.

Though storms may come and shadows loom,
Each bend reveals a fragrant bloom.
Untold stories of joy and pain,
In every challenge, wisdom gained.

The Domain of Memory

In gardens lush, where thoughts reside,
Memories bloom, like petals wide.
Time stands still, a fragrant breath,
In whispered dreams, we conquer death.

Old photographs, faces fade,
Yet in our hearts, their love's remade.
Songs of laughter echo clear,
The domain of what we hold dear.

Unraveled threads of distant years,
Woven with smiles, bound with tears.
Each moment captured, bright and bold,
Stories cherished, forever told.

Through fog and mist, we'll find our way,
To places where our spirits stay.
In every heartbeat, memories dance,
In the silence, an everlasting chance.

A labyrinth of Dreams

In shadows deep, we wander wide,
Through twisting paths that time can hide.
A whisper of hope, a flicker of light,
We chase the echoes of the night.

Each turn a choice, a secret door,
In this maze where hearts explore.
Lost in thoughts that drift and sway,
We find our way, come what may.

With every heartbeat, a new refrain,
A dance of joy, a hint of pain.
In dreams we weave, so pure, so bright,
A labyrinth in the mind's soft light.

Through every corner, stories told,
Of love and fear, of young and old.
Though paths may twist, we hold on tight,
In a labyrinth built by our own sight.

So take my hand as we roam far,
Guided by wishes, like a distant star.
For in this dream, we are not alone,
In the labyrinth of dreams, we have found home.

The Chipped Pottery of Love

In sunlight's glow, the cracks are bare,
Each flaw a mark of tender care.
The chipped edges tell a tale,
Of moments sweet that still prevail.

With gentle hands, we mend and form,
Through stormy nights, our hearts stayed warm.
The beauty lies in what we share,
In pottery of love, beyond compare.

Though seasons change and time may wear,
We hold the fragility with great flair.
In every piece, a memory lives,
A testament to all love gives.

Together we paint, with colors bright,
Filling the cracks with bold delight.
Each imperfection, a treasure found,
In the chipped pottery, love's profound.

So let us cherish this crafted art,
For in each fragment lies a heart.
As years go by and seasons flow,
In this chipped pottery, our love will grow.

Colors of a Faded Canvas

Once vibrant hues, now tones of gray,
The artist's dreams have slipped away.
Brush strokes soft, yet edges worn,
A canvas sings of love reborn.

In whispers of what used to be,
The colors dance, wild and free.
Though faded now, their spirit glows,
In every line, a memory shows.

The palette holds a history bright,
Of laughter shared and dreams in flight.
Yet in the stillness, shadows play,
A reminder of the bright array.

Through layers thick of joy and pain,
The hues emerge, like gentle rain.
In every drop, a tale unfolds,
Of colors bright and stories told.

So let the canvas find its muse,
In every shade, love's intricate hues.
For even faded, it still inspires,
In the colors of dreams, we find our fires.

Drifting Through Dismal Skies

On clouds of gray, we float and sway,
In search of light, we drift away.
The winds may howl, the rain may fall,
Yet hope remains through it all.

With heavy hearts, we brave the storm,
In dismal skies, our spirits warm.
Through thunder's roar and lightning's spark,
We find our way, igniting the dark.

Each drop a tear, each gust a sigh,
Yet love abides as we soar high.
For in the gloom, a flicker glows,
A beacon bright amidst our woes.

As we drift on, hand in hand,
Together we face this endless land.
In dismal skies, our dreams take flight,
With hope as our guide, we chase the light.

So let us wander through the gray,
And dance with shadows come what may.
For even in darkness, our hearts can rise,
As we drift through dismal skies.

Wistful Memories

In the quiet of the night,
Whispers from days gone by,
Echoes of laughter linger,
Beneath the autumn sky.

Faded photographs tell stories,
Moments that time forgot,
Fraying threads of happiness,
Now woven in a knot.

Each smile captured in stillness,
A longing for what has passed,
The warmth of those embraces,
In shadows, they are cast.

Walking through familiar places,
The scent of pine and dew,
Reminds me of those journeys,
And what once felt so true.

Yet in this realm of memories,
A bittersweet refrain,
I cherish every heartbeat,
Even through the pain.

Weathered Edges of Yesterday

Pages torn from the books,
Tales of love and loss,
Ink that bleeds with sorrow,
Every circle, every cross.

Skies of gray above me,
Reflect the days once bright,
Where dreams danced in the sunset,
Now fade into the night.

Rusty swings in the playground,
Echoes of a child's voice,
Every laughter, every tear,
A ghostly, fleeting choice.

Paths we wandered together,
Now silent, overgrown,
Yet in the heart's deep chamber,
Those moments are my own.

Weathered edges, soft whispers,
Memories held so tight,
In the tapestry of living,
They shine through the night.

The Ashes of What Was

Fires once burned brightly,
Now embers fade away,
What was once a roaring blaze,
Is just a dull array.

Chasing shadows, remnants lost,
In the corners of the mind,
Fragments of our laughter,
In ashes, intertwined.

We built a world of wonder,
With dreams both bold and grand,
Yet here the smoke still lingers,
Scattered through shifting sand.

Each memory a phoenix,
Rising from silent dust,
Though what I sought has vanished,
In the past, I still trust.

From the ashes, new beginnings,
Will bloom within the strife,
Through the loss and longing,
I search for hope in life.

Underneath the Surface

Beneath the waves of silence,
The currents pull and sway,
Hidden depths of sorrow,
Where shadows often play.

Glimmers of the sun above,
Dancing on the tide,
Yet here below, the quiet,
Where secrets like to hide.

The weight of unspoken feelings,
Like stones that drag me down,
Yearning for the light above,
In silence, I might drown.

Whispers echo in caverns deep,
Where no one else can see,
Every pulse, a question,
Of who I'm meant to be.

Yet if I dive beneath the hurt,
With courage as my guide,
I'll find a voice worth sharing,
Beneath the surface, wide.

Phantom Rhythms of the Heart

In shadows where whispers play,
A pulse beats soft, yet far away.
Dreams linger like ghosts at night,
Filling the void with flickering light.

Echoes dance through silent halls,
As passion rises, then gently falls.
Each heartbeat speaks, a secret tune,
In a world where hearts are out of tune.

Lost in the depths of a lover's gaze,
The elegance of time begins to blaze.
Yet hidden beneath the veil of grace,
A phantom rhythm we constantly chase.

Beneath the stars, we find our way,
In the silence where dreams dare sway.
With every breath, the rhythm grows,
A melody only the heart knows.

So let us waltz in twilight's glow,
Where phantom rhythms softly flow.
From dusk till dawn, we'll never part,
Together in this dance of heart.

A Symphony of Broken Chords

Strummed strings beneath the sky,
Whispers of melodies that pass by.
Once vibrant notes now out of reach,
Each silence is a lesson we teach.

In this symphony of loss and strife,
Every chord reflects a piece of life.
Fingers tremble on the fretted lines,
Creating beauty where the heart confines.

Gone are the harmonies we knew,
Replaced by echoes, haunting and true.
Yet in the void, we search for light,
As broken chords ignite the night.

With every strain, a tear we shed,
Each memory a word left unsaid.
But from chaos, new songs arise,
In brokenness, our spirit flies.

So let us find our way to play,
In dissonance, we'll weave our stay.
A symphony of scars transformed,
In broken chords, a new love warmed.

Scattered Petals on a Forgotten Path

Upon the ground, the colors fade,
Petals strewn where shadows wade.
Once vibrant blooms in summer's kiss,
Now whispers of a fleeting bliss.

Every step on this lonely trail,
A fragrant hint of tales regale.
Ghostly whispers of laughter ring,
In the breeze, the past takes wing.

Beneath the trees, the petals dance,
Remnants of love and lost romance.
Each step a sigh, each sigh a tear,
As echoes of time weave memories clear.

Yet in the stillness, hope remains,
Resilience through the softest pains.
With every petal, we find our way,
To cherish moments, come what may.

So gather these fragments on the ground,
In scattered petals, life is found.
For every loss, a seed is sown,
On forgotten paths, we wander on.

The Light Beyond the Tattered Veil

Through layers worn and threads undone,
A flicker shines; we seek the sun.
Tattered veils speak of days gone by,
Yet whispers of hope, they still imply.

In every tear, a story glows,
Reflecting all the love we chose.
With trembling hands, we part the seams,
To uncover reality woven from dreams.

The heart beats in a rhythm bright,
Guided softly by that distant light.
Though shadows linger, we dare to see,
A vision of what we long to be.

And as we draw the fabric near,
The truths within begin to clear.
With faith, we step into the haze,
Embracing the light that ever stays.

So lift the veil, let courage soar,
For beyond the dark, lies so much more.
In every thread, the promise dwells,
The light beyond our tattered shells.

Fractured Melodies

In shadows where the music plays,
Notes scatter like lost dreams,
Whispers linger in the haze,
Fractured chords unravel seams.

Echoes dance on broken strings,
Faint reminders of what was bright,
Hope within the silence clings,
Guiding hearts through endless night.

A symphony of silent tears,
Each note a tale, each pause a sigh,
Carving paths through hidden fears,
Melodies that never die.

The fall of night brings gentle grace,
Softly cradling the pain we share,
In every tune, a silent space,
A fractured song, beyond compare.

Yet in the chaos, beauty finds,
Resilience born from quiet strife,
Within the heart, a song unwinds,
Fractured tunes of vibrant life.

Glimmers of Distant Smiles

Across the miles, a smile glows,
Warming hearts through the endless sea,
In fleeting moments, friendship grows,
A thread of light connecting we.

Through crowded paths and bustling dreams,
Glimmers spark in the darkest nights,
Each laughter shared, a river streams,
Reflecting joy in gentle flights.

Time may stretch like shadows long,
Yet memories stitch the frayed seams,
With every note, we weave our song,
Carried forth on the wings of dreams.

Distance fades beneath soft skies,
When shared stories bridge the gap,
In hidden depths, love never lies,
Glimmers of peace in a world's map.

So let us cherish these bright sparks,
Illuminate paths through the unknown,
In distant smiles, the heart embarks,
Together, yet never alone.

The Weight of Unspoken Words

Beneath the silence, tension brews,
Words linger like heavy clouds,
Each thought a feather, colored blues,
Yet voices tremble, lost in crowds.

In every glance, a story waits,
Unraveled truths hide in the dark,
Hearts speak volumes, crossed by fates,
An echo forged from a silent spark.

The burdens borne on teetering lips,
Unshed tears pool in waiting eyes,
As hope within the shadows slips,
Time weaves dreams into goodbyes.

Yet still we crave the echoes near,
To bridge the chasm, hearts collide,
In honesty, we'll learn to steer,
The weight of words we must not hide.

So gather courage, break the chains,
Let whispers flow like morning dew,
For in the sharing, love remains,
The weight of truth makes us anew.

Tangled in Yesterday's Echo

Lost in the weave of time's embrace,
Yesterday's echo lingers still,
Memories dance in a shadowed space,
Filling hearts with bittersweet thrill.

Threads entangle like a woven lie,
Each moment a stitch from the past,
In every sigh, a silent cry,
The fleeting days are shadows cast.

Yet in the knots, we find a thread,
A pathway home to the light we seek,
For in the stories that we've read,
Is strength to heal the lost and weak.

Reflections flicker in fading light,
Guiding us through the thickened mist,
As dawn approaches, soft and bright,
Yesterday's echoes hold their tryst.

So let us cherish what we may,
In tangled roots, we find our way,
For every echo that fades away,
Builds tomorrow from yesterday.

Shards of Sentiment

Fragments of whispers in the night,
Glimmers of hope in a fading light.
Memories linger, delicate and fine,
Echoes of laughter, forever entwined.

Promises made, now dust in the air,
Torn pages of stories we used to share.
Yet in the silence, your voice still calls,
A tender reminder, despite the falls.

Shattered reflections of what used to be,
Each piece a story, each shard a plea.
In the mosaic of dreams, we find our place,
Amidst the shadows, a lingering grace.

Time has a way of shaping our days,
Carving our paths in intricate ways.
Love leaves its mark, both bitter and sweet,
In the shards of sentiment, we find our feet.

The heart's resilience, a beacon of light,
Guiding us through the relentless night.
Together we stand, though apart we roam,
In the shards of sentiment, we find our home.

Scattered Embers of Emotion

Flickers of warmth in the coldest night,
Scattered embers, a soft, gentle light.
Each memory glows, a fire once bright,
In the remnants of love, shadows take flight.

Whispers of passion that dance in the air,
Ghosts of connection, too fragile to bear.
The warmth of your smile, a sweet memory,
In every heartbeat, you're still a part of me.

Time tends the fire, with care and with grace,
But embers can fade, leaving just a trace.
Yet in the ashes, a spark can ignite,
A chance for revival, a flicker of bright.

Scattered like stars in the wide open sky,
Emotions unspoken, we let them fly.
Each ember a token of moments we saved,
In the scattered remnants, our hearts are paved.

Through the echoes of sorrow, beauty can bloom,
Finding light in the dark, dispelling the gloom.
In the scattered embers, our stories live on,
A flame of remembrance, never truly gone.

A Tapestry of Lost Promises

Threads of our dreams, woven with care,
Stitched in the fabric of moments we share.
Yet, as time weaves, some colors may fade,
A tapestry rich, but frayed at the braid.

Stolen glances and secrets we'd keep,
In the folds of the fabric, where sorrows sleep.
Promises whispered in the dark of the night,
Left unfulfilled, now lost to our sight.

Woven with laughter, adorned with our pain,
Every connection a beautiful gain.
But the loom of the past spins tales of regret,
In the tapestry's weave, our hearts would bet.

Moments in time that once brightly glowed,
Now threads of uncertainty, heavy and load.
Yet in each stitch, there's a story to tell,
Of love that was vibrant, of wishing you well.

A tapestry made of both joy and despair,
Crafted with passion, frayed by the air.
Though promises lost may not always remain,
In the fabric of life, our love is the grain.

Bittersweet Remnants of Us

In the quiet of dusk, shadows unfold,
Bittersweet remnants of stories retold.
Fragments of laughter, tears we once cried,
In the corners of memory, love could not hide.

The taste of your kiss still lingers on me,
Like wine on the lips, a taste of history.
Moments that shimmer with both joy and pain,
In the bittersweet echoes, our hearts still remain.

Paths intertwined in the sands of our time,
Dancing in rhythm, our souls in their prime.
Yet tides carry whispers of seasons gone by,
In the remnants of us, the heart still will try.

Through the laughter and heartache, lessons we
learned,\nIn the warmth of connection, forever burned.
Each scar a reminder of love's gentle touch,
In the bittersweet remnants, we've cherished so much.

A melody haunting, both tender and real,
Notes of our journey, the lessons they heal.
In the bittersweet beauty of all that we've lost,
We find our foundation, despite all the cost.

Scattered Memories

Whispers of laughter hang in the air,
Dusty old photos, a time to share.
Flickering moments, so vivid, yet frail,
Elusive echoes where dreams set sail.

Fragments of joy, both bitter and sweet,
Chasing the shadows where lost faces meet.
In corners of rooms where silence resides,
Each breath tells stories that time cannot hide.

Tattered postcards from places we roamed,
A world once vibrant, now feels like a home.
Colors of memories, faded and worn,
In the heart's gallery, all too well adorned.

Ghosts of the past with each passing glance,
Live in the spaces where we once danced.
And though they may scatter like leaves in the breeze,
They root in the soul, reminding with ease.

Memories linger like stars in the night,
They guide us through shadows, they spark up the light.
In the tapestry woven with threads of our years,
Scattered but cherished, they conquer our fears.

Mosaic of Longing

Pieces of dreams, strewn on the floor,
Colors of wishes, an aching encore.
Fragments of hope, in a swirling array,
A mosaic of longing in hues of dismay.

Each shard a moment, each hue a desire,
Treatment of heartache ignites like a fire.
Yearning for futures that flicker and fade,
Crafted from blessings, whispered, delayed.

Faces of strangers, reflections unknown,
Mirroring yearnings that solitude's grown.
Infinite patterns that draw us apart,
Yet bind us together—they speak from the heart.

Love's gentle touch mingles with ache,
In this tapestry woven, a chance we can take.
Caught in the visage of dreams long pursued,
A mosaic of longing, forever renewed.

Through shadows we wander, in search of the light,
Each piece a memory, soft glimmers bright.
In the chaos of fragments, hope softly sings,
A mosaic of longing, with all that it brings.

Shards of Yesterday

Shattered reflections, a broken glass,
Fragments of the past that swiftly amass.
Each piece a story, a member of time,
Shrouded in silence, in rhythm and rhyme.

Faded photographs, whispers of old,
Treasured remains of the moments we hold.
Shards of connection slip through our hands,
Carving our journeys, weaving new strands.

In alleys of memory, shadows will play,
Echoes of laughter that never decay.
Lost upon highways where dreams intertwine,
Fragments of yesterday, eternally shine.

Textures of longing etched on the heart,
Bridges of time that will never depart.
Through broken edges, we search for a way,
Finding the beauty in disarray.

With every sharp corner, adventures unfold,
Tales of resilience and courage retold.
Through shards of yesterday, we learn to embrace,
The mosaic of life, with its delicate grace.

Reflections in a Distant Sea

Waves lap softly on a silent shore,
Echoing whispers of days long before.
Reflections of dreams dance on the tide,
Carried by currents where secrets abide.

Shells filled with stories, each grain a thought,
Tides pull away what the heart has sought.
In the vast expanse where horizons blend,
Reflections of longing, a journey without end.

Sunsets paint skies with colors so bold,
Each hue a promise, a memory told.
In the depths of the waters, a mirror shines clear,
Inviting the dreams that still linger near.

Moonlight caresses the waves as they swell,
Carrying wishes that time cannot quell.
In the rhythm of waters, past meets the now,
Reflections in a distant sea show us how.

So sail through the waves, let your spirit roam,
In the embrace of the sea, you may find home.
For every reflection, a story starts anew,
In the depths of the ocean, your heart will break through.

Reverberations of a Forgotten Tune

In shadows whisper echoes frail,
Notes of laughter, soft and pale.
Once a song that filled the air,
Now lost in time, beyond compare.

A melody that haunts the night,
Drifting gently, out of sight.
Each chord a memory, bittersweet,
Dancing leaves beneath my feet.

The rhythm of the heartbeats race,
Faintly tracing love's embrace.
In the silence, it will play,
A forgotten tune, fading away.

Yet in the stillness, there's a spark,
A lingering note when days are dark.
It calls to souls, so lost in time,
To remember love, to make it rhyme.

Though years may turn the pages worn,
A spark of hope, forever born.
Let the echoes find their way,
In the heart, they'll always stay.

The Cracked Canvas of Desire

With strokes of passion, colors blend,
Each hue a hope, around the bend.
Yet cracks emerge, a restless cry,
Dreams forgotten, slowly die.

An artist's gaze can see the fray,
Where once was light, now shadows play.
The yearning blooms with every sigh,
A heart's reflection, asking why.

In distant corners, whispers dwell,
Secrets locked in silken shell.
The brush untamed, a wish to mend,
Fingers trace where passions bend.

Yet love remains a fleeting dance,
Fragile moments, not by chance.
In every flaw, a story told,
Of longing that just won't grow old.

Thus on this frame, I find my trespass,
In every crack, a moment passed.
To restore the beauty scarred by fate,
To understand, to celebrate.

Heartstrings Unraveled

Threads of gold entwined with care,
Woven stories, love laid bare.
Yet time applies its weary hand,
And unravels what we had planned.

Each tug a memory, sharp and bright,
Pulling at hearts, both day and night.
Frayed edges brush against the soul,
In tangled knots, we lose control.

A symphony of feelings clash,
Moments captured, gone in a flash.
In every snare, a vibrant hue,
A canvas rich with me and you.

Though threads may fray and sometimes break,
In each small tear, new paths awake.
For in the spaces left behind,
Resilience blooms, forever kind.

Let heartstrings echo in the void,
A gentle reminder, love enjoyed.
Unraveled paths can intertwine,
In tender ways, our hearts align.

Whispered Longings

In twilight's hush, a secret stirs,
Soft as a breeze that lightly purrs.
In shadows deep, desires bloom,
Cradled softly in the room.

Words unsaid, like fragile lace,
Woven dreams in delicate space.
Each sigh a promise, barely heard,
Lingering whispers, history stirred.

The moon reveals what daylight hides,
A tender truth that love abides.
In silence shared, our spirits meet,
Entwined together, incomplete.

Longings drift on the evening air,
Crafting verses for those who dare.
Each heartbeat resonates as one,
In whispered dreams, our journey's begun.

With every pause, the world stands still,
A fleeting moment, a lover's thrill.
In the night's embrace, hearts align,
Whispered longings, forever entwined.

Soft Scraps of a Hidden Truth

Whispers dance upon the breeze,
Secrets tucked beneath the trees.
Glimmers of what we fear to share,
Soft scraps linger in the air.

Shadows tremble, truth concealed,
Hearts undone, yet never healed.
Threads of hope weave through despair,
Faint echoes linger everywhere.

In silence, stories start to bloom,
Unspoken words in every room.
Fragments of a life once bright,
Now worn by the fading light.

A tapestry of dreams once spun,
Dances with the setting sun.
Each stitch holds a secret tight,
Bound by the fabric of the night.

And though we hide, we seek the way,
To touch the dawn beyond the gray.
In scraps we find what lies beneath,
The hidden truths that bring us peace.

The Silent Garden of Tomorrow

In quiet corners, shadows play,
Gentle whispers greet the day.
Petals droop, collecting dew,
In this garden, life feels new.

With every breeze, the hopes arise,
Beneath the vast and open skies.
Seeds of promise, soft and rare,
Blooming softly, unaware.

Time flows gently through the leaves,
Woven tales that heart believes.
Every bud holds dreams untold,
In silence, futures start to unfold.

The twilight brings a tender hush,
As day gives way to softening blush.
Underneath the crescent glow,
The silent garden starts to grow.

With every star, a wish is sown,
In this quiet place, we're never alone.
Tomorrow whispers on the breeze,
In the garden of forgotten dreams.

A Patchwork of Regret

Stitched together with frayed seams,
A tapestry of broken dreams.
Each square tells of choices made,
In colors that quietly fade.

Moments lost in wishful sighs,
Reflections hidden in our eyes.
Faded memories linger still,
Chasing shadows up the hill.

In every fold, the weight of time,
The echoes of a distant chime.
Hearts once woven in warm embrace,
Now unraveling, lost in space.

Through patchwork pain, we learn to grow,
In fragile pieces, truth can show.
Gathered fragments under the light,
Illuminate the darkest night.

And though regret may leave its trace,
It's but a part of life's embrace.
In every tear, a lesson bled,
A patchwork quilt of what we've said.

Worn Pages of a Love Story

Faded lines tell tales of yore,
Whispered dreams behind each door.
Hands once held, now feel the loss,
In the margins, love's heavy cost.

Ink runs deep through every page,
Captured moments of joy and rage.
Stories dwell in shadows cast,
Worn like memories that last.

Each chapter holds a tender tale,
Of passion's fire and quietail.
Through laughter, heartache, joy, and tears,
These pages speak of countless fears.

Bookmarks hidden in the haste,
Of rushing days that cannot waste.
Yet still they wait, those worn pages,
To tell of love through all life's stages.

As time unfolds, each bond will bend,
Yet in the heart, stories extend.
Worn pages hold a timeless grace,
A love story we still embrace.

www.ingramcontent.com/pod-product-compliance
Ingram Content Group UK Ltd.
Pitfield, Milton Keynes, MK11 3LW, UK
UKHW021419230125
4262UKWH00028B/373